WEIRDO 2

EVEN WEIRDER!

ISBN 978-93-5471-070-4

Printed in India at Polykam offset New Delhi 110028
first printing 2019
This edition : December 2021
Typeset in Chaloops Senior, Push Ups, and Lunch Box

ANH DO

Illustrated by JULES FABER

WEIRDO 2
EVEN WEIRDER!

SCHOLASTIC INC.

BLOCK HEAD!

CHAPTER 1

I was out shopping for a **birthday present** for the seventh-best-looking girl in the class. So why did I have five years' worth of **toilet paper** in the cart?

Because

my life is
weird.

If something's on sale at the store, Mom will buy **lots** of it.

And guess what was on sale today?

That's right,

toilet paper.

There we all were . . . looking like

the family that has the

MOST POOS

in the world.

The fact is, we don't just use toilet paper in the bathroom. We use it for other **stuff** around the house . . .

Like **blowing** your nose.

Wiping up **spills**.

Ten pin bowling.

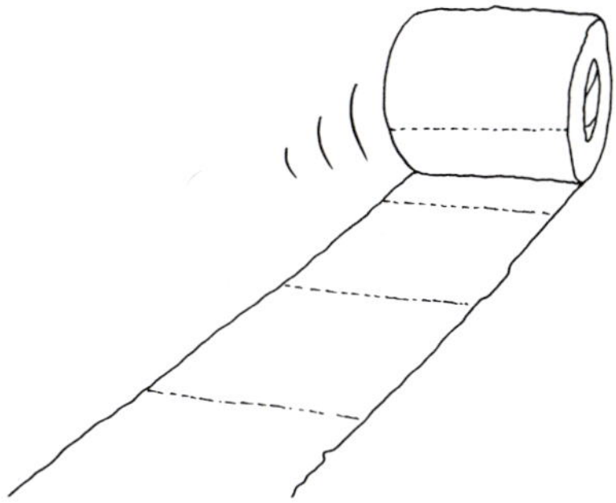

Did I tell you my mom was **thrifty**? She's one of those people who gets a little too excited about the lady in the corner of the shop giving out the **free sausage samples**.

Mom will make us **all line up** for a taste, no matter what the sample is.

PICKLED PORK CHOPS?
YES, PLEASE!

WOULD YOU LIKE TO TRY OUR NEW SPICY SAUSAGE?

You're only allowed **one** sausage per person, but Mom makes us walk away and then come back looking slightly different, just to get **more food**.

And if the sausages are **REALLY tasty**, she'll make us come back one **extra time**.

Roger's **the worst** at shopping. Somehow **strange stuff** always ends up in the cart when he's around.

guilty
BUTT
WHO BOUGHT THIS ITCHY BUTT CREAM?
guilty

Anyway, there we were at the checkout with our

2,000

rolls of toilet paper, when I looked across and saw . . . **BELLA ALLEN!**

"What are you buying?" she asked.

"We're just buying a . . . birthday present for you," I replied.

"Is that my present behind your back?" she asked with a smile.

"Oh, no, that isn't for you either."

I brought out the **itchy butt cream** to show her.

"Okaaaaay, bye, Weir," she said.

NOOOOO!

Now Bella Allen thinks I am **the king of poop**. That I need a cart full of toilet paper all for myself!

Can my life get any **worse?**

My life **just got worse!**

Now the **whole** supermarket's looking at me!

How did the lady at the checkout know my name? Must have been

a lucky guess!

BUURR
RRRRP!

CHAPTER 2

My first name is **Weir**. My last name is **Do**. (Yep, rhymes with "go.")

Just in case you missed my first book, let me tell you a little bit about me and my family.

You already know I'm a **bit weird**. Like when they handed out **talents**, I wound up with . . .

And when they handed out **family hobbies** . . .

And you already know that my mom is thrifty. She **really** is.

For **Roger's birthday**, instead of paying for **real** helium balloons that float up to the ceiling . . .

. . . she just blew up plain balloons and then **stuck** them to the ceiling with **sticky tape**.

She's also one of those moms who makes us wear **hand-me-down** clothes. I got stuck with Sally's **old school shoes** . . . but at least I didn't get her sweater!

My sister, Sally, is **super** neat. She does

everything perfectly.

She even peels an orange all in **one go**.

And she's really good at making things, like **balloon** animals.

Sally **never** makes a mess eating her noodles.

But me, I always seem to get that one long noodle that goes on and on forever!

At least I'm not as **messy** as Roger. Sometimes he even ends up with noodles **coming out of his nose**.

Roger is my little brother, and he likes to **destroy stuff**. This week he's been **throwing** things into the bath. To **"clean"** them.

Often important things . . .

CLEAN!

CLEAN!
BREAD

Mom refused to waste the soggy bread . . . and I have to say, the **soggy sandwich** was one of the **worst three sandwiches** I've ever had in my life.

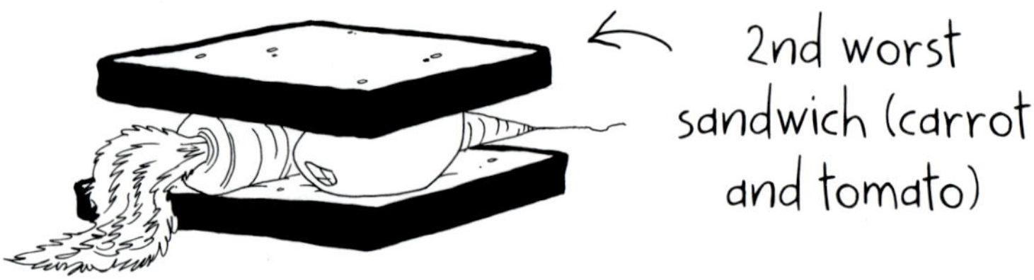

My dad is **just plain strange**.

He can do a **burp** that lasts for a looooooooooooooooooooooooooooooooooooooooooooooooooooooooooooooooooooooooooooooooong time!

BUU

UUURRR

still going!

R R R

RRRRRP

finally finished!

Dad can also **fart** from the **front door** to the **back door**, but we won't go into that.

The other thing Dad likes to do is **dance really badly**. He tries to copy people on TV.

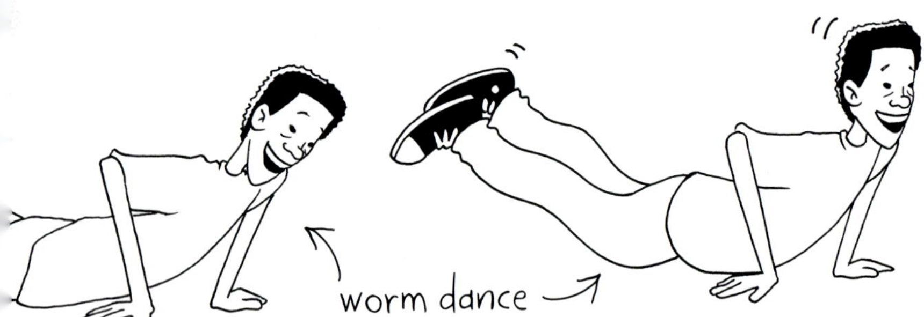

robot dance

still the
worm dance

Finally, there's Granddad. His teeth come out, and his body parts make **funny** noises . . .

And he likes to play **silly** tricks.

ZZZZZ
ZZZZZ
ZZZZZZ!

HA HA HA
HA HA HA HA HA

He also pulls his pants up **really high**, which is the opposite of some of the **cool** kids at school.

Even our **pet bird** is weird. Most birds like to make happy chirpy noises. But **Blockhead** always makes strange sounds, like . . .

WOOF WOOF!

And sometimes . . .

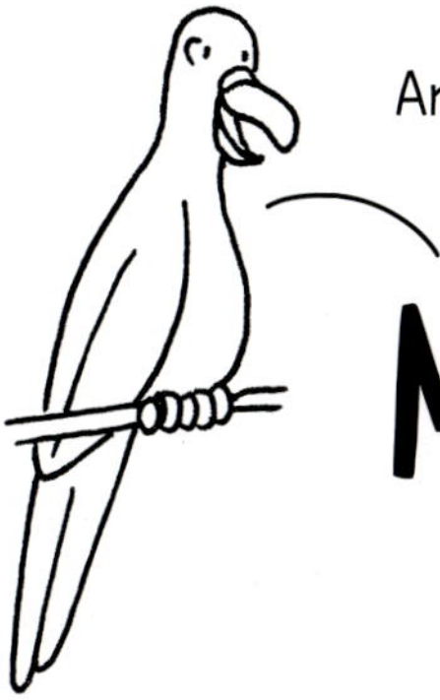

MOOO!

And if he's eaten some **funny birdseed**, he'll say . . .

WANNA FIGHT?

Henry's my best friend from school. He doesn't care that I'm weird, or that I like to draw silly pictures.

Like this one . . .

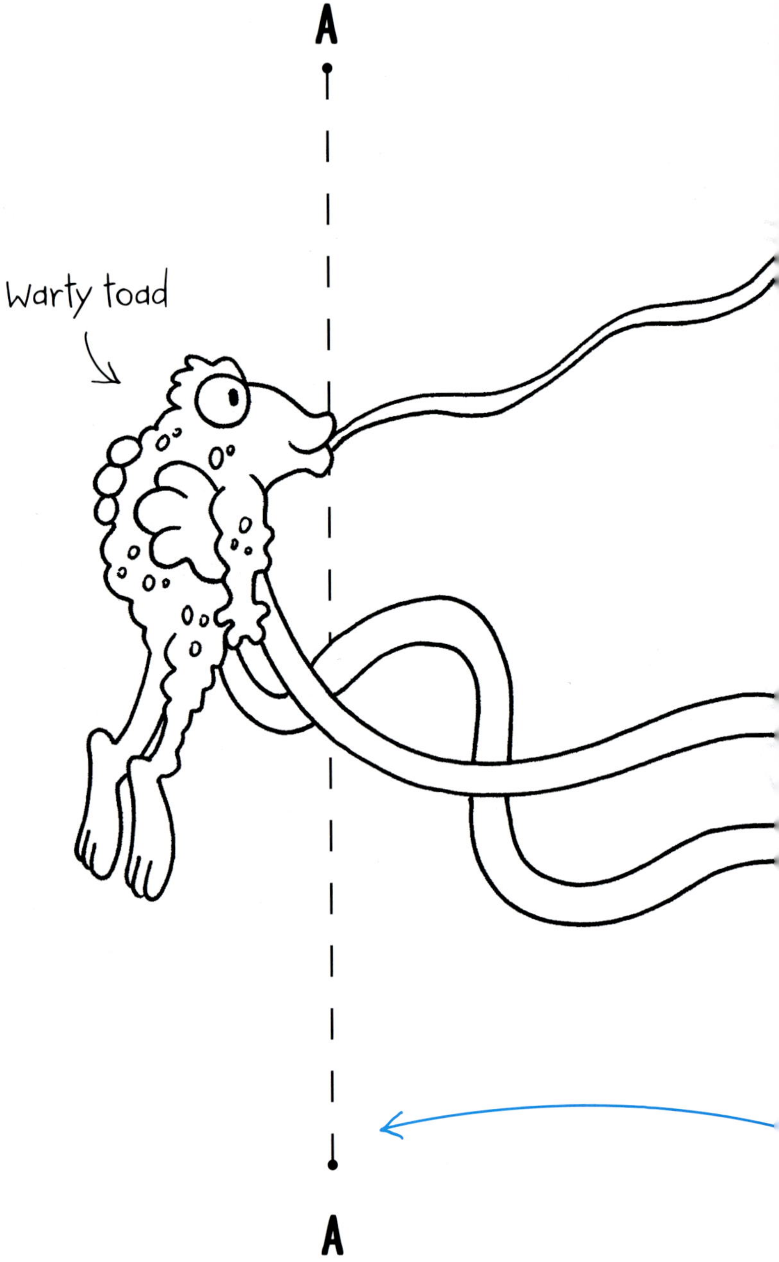
A
Warty toad
A

B
Blake
Fold line B over
to meet line A
B

Me and Henry like to make up new words for things, too . . . like **"Finkles."**

That's the word we invented for the **wrinkles** you get on your **fingers** when you've sat in the bath

for

too

long.

We think if we say it enough everyone will start to use it,

even the queen.

CHAPTER 3

Bella's party is two days away, so I want to be as **normal** as possible at school to make sure that she won't **un-invite** me.

This was going to be hard since today we were going on a school trip to the **zoo** and Granddad was coming as a teacher's helper.

I knew it was going to be **trouble** when Granddad showed up at breakfast wearing fake **monkey ears**.

When we got on the **school bus**, Granddad took the empty seat next to Henry, and the only seat left for me was next to . . .

Bella.

I like Bella. I like her **a lot**. But I'm not sure if I'm ready to sit next to her on the bus.

We said hi . . .

. . . **and that's it!**

I didn't know what else to say to her. She didn't know what else to say to me. We just sat there **staring** at the back of the heads of the people in front of us!

The sight of Granddad's **monkey ears** and Henry's **fuzzy orange hair** gave me an idea.

I took out my sketchbook and started **drawing** . . .

"What are you drawing?" Bella asked.

Bella reached down into her bag and pulled out a pair of **glasses**. She put them on and looked closely at my drawing.

I hadn't seen Bella wearing glasses before, and I must have been staring at them, because she noticed.

"The glasses are new," said Bella. "The eye doctor said I need to wear them when I'm looking at something closely."

"**Cool**," I said. "Can I try them on?"

She took them off and put them on **me**.

The glasses made **everything** look different.

They made Granddad's ears look

even bigger.

And Henry's head was **HUGE!**

You **do not** want to know what Toby Hogan looked like . . .

That was when Bella asked me to **draw** her.

YES!

This was my chance to **impress** Bella with the one thing that I'm

really good at!

I picked up my sketchbook and pencil and started drawing Bella as well as I could.

When I finished, I showed her the picture of herself.

Bella said it was nice, but I don't think she meant it, because she had the same look on her face that Mom had when she found that **dead mouse** in the laundry basket . . .

Then I realized . . .

Oh no!

I **forgot** to take off the glasses, and they made me draw her **really badly**!

Oh man . . . What a way to start the day.

DUCK!

CHAPTER 4

When we got to the **zoo**, the first animals we saw were the **monkeys**.

I love monkeys, so me and Granddad went right up close to the fence.

I thought Granddad's monkey ears looked **silly**, but the monkeys must have thought they looked **real**, because the first thing that happened was

a monkey

threw a banana

right at Granddad!

Granddad **ducked** out of the way.

Then I **ducked** out of the way.

And the **banana** hit Henry . . .

right in the face!

It was sooo funny, I started laughing.

HAHA!!!!!!!

I was **laughing**

so hard

I didn't see the **second banana** that was thrown.

Bella ducked it.

Blake **ducked** it.

Toby Hogan **ducked** it.

And it hit **me** right on the side of the head!

Now **everyone** was laughing at **me**!

Even Granddad!

I guess it looked **pretty funny**!

As Henry and me stood there **flicking** the banana off ourselves, a whole bunch of **ducks** ran up to eat the bits off the ground.

They were funny, those ducks. Fat ones, skinny ones, and a big spotty one.

The **spotty** one had three little ducklings following it,

which was **very cute**.

Bella gave me a **hanky** to wipe myself. "Here you go, Weir," she said.

"Thanks," I said. And that's when I realized the hanky had **little frogs** on it.

I looked up, and Bella was **smiling**.

Soon it was lunchtime, which was perfect, because I had heaps of ideas for **cool animal pictures**. First I tried a

giraffe and a **kangaroo**.

A **zebra** and an **elephant** . . .

A **panda** and a **gorilla** . . .

But then I decided I wanted to try another drawing of Bella. I quickly drew her while she watched Henry

pretending he was a

sea lion.

I was pretty happy with my drawing and knew Bella would like it much more than the last one.

But as I went to hand it to her,

the **skinny duck** waddled over and

snatched it

away from me! »»

Before I knew it, Bella had jumped up and was chasing after the duck with my drawing in its bill!

I ran after her.

I might have mentioned that I'm **not** a very fast runner . . .

And it turns out that duck was a

very fast waddler!

We chased that duck down past

the **gorilla** enclosure,

through the **bat** cave, »»

along the **penguin** pool . . . »»

But then we lost the duck around the **meerkat** bend.

Not only had we lost the duck, but now **we were lost**, too!

We couldn't find Granddad, Miss Franklin, or anyone from school . . .

so we found **the next BEST thing** . . .

"Hey," said Bella, "what are you going to wear to **my party**?"

Huh? I thought to myself.

"Oh yeah," I replied. "Sure . . . I'm going to go as . . ."

A FROG!
COOL!

"So what was your drawing of, anyway?" asked Bella.

"Oh, nothing," I replied. "Just an—"

"**BELLA ALLEN!**" the zoo loudspeaker suddenly boomed.

"**AND WEIRDO!**" the loudspeaker continued.

Everyone at the zoo laughed.

All the animals, too.

The **monkeys** . . .

The **penguins** . . .

Even the **duck** with the **glasses**!

I wanted to run away and hide, but before I could make a move, Granddad appeared.

The day at the zoo

wasn't a complete disaster.

On my way out, I found the *perfect* **birthday present** for Bella in the gift shop . . .

TWO ROBOTS

CHAPTER 5

At school the next day, Miss Franklin told us that we all needed to draw a **picture** of someone else in the class.

Here was my chance to draw Bella again!

But then Bella asked **Henry** if **he** would be her partner!

WHAT?
WANT TO DRAW EACH OTHER?
SURE!

So I wound up with Clare instead . . .

I thought I'd done a

pretty good job

of my **drawing**.

Henry's drawing of Bella was **even worse** than mine from the bus!

After school, Henry invited me over to his place to work on our **costumes** for Bella's party.

Henry was going as a **computer**. He put a box on his head, and I helped him attach a keyboard to his chest. When we finished, he looked like a human iPad.

He had lots of green cardboard for me to use to make a frog hat.

Perfect!

When we were finished, Henry showed me his **COLLECTION OF ROCKS** that he'd made to look like things . . .

. . . and then he introduced me to his sister.

JANE.

JANE!
JANE!

OH, HI, HENRY!
JANE, THIS IS WEIR DO!

"WEIRDO?" said Jane. "That's not very nice."

"Oh, no, that's his name," said Henry.

"Yeah, it's actually my name," I said.

Then I met Henry's twin brothers. They looked **exactly** the same!

"I can see that," I said.

They even **talked** the same.

I couldn't tell them apart!

WE ARE DIFFERENT IN SOME WAYS, THOUGH.

WE ARE DIFFERENT IN SOME WAYS, THOUGH.

HE LIKES TO EAT GREEN M&M'S.
AND I LIKE TO EAT BLUE M&M'S.

YEAH, HE LIKES TO EAT BLUE M&M'S, AND I LIKE TO EAT GREEN M&M'S.

It was like looking at **two robots**.

Then Henry's mom and dad and their dog came out.

So this is what a **normal family** looks like!

"It's dinnertime, boys," said Mr. O'Henry. "Come join us at the table."

My mom's and dad's dinners **never** look how they're supposed to.

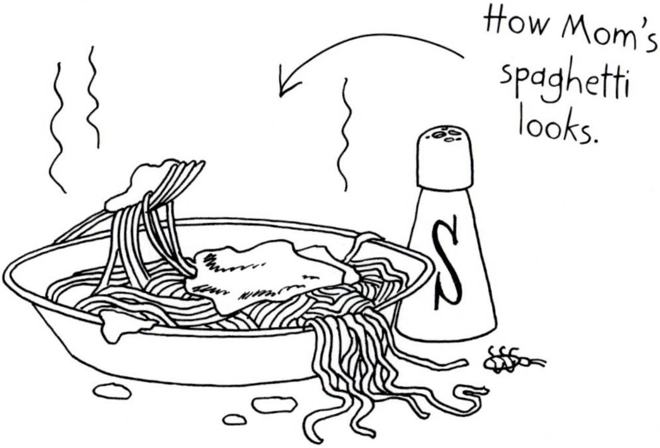

How a Sunday dinner is supposed to look.

How Dad's Sunday dinner looks.

. . . but they **always** taste **delicious**!

But Mrs. O'Henry's roast looked **just like** the picture in the book!

This is going to be **SUPER yummy**, I thought to myself.

Shame it **tasted** like **cardboard**!

BIG CUCUMBER!

CHAPTER 6

Today is Bella's **birthday party**!

Bella's present is wrapped . . .

and my **green** clothes are ready . . .

My **frog** hat is—

"**HEY**," I said, "where's my frog hat?"

Then I heard a

TERRIBLE

SPLASH!

coming from the **bathroom**.

ROGER!

NOOOOO

I ran to the bathroom, but it was **too late**.
My frog hat was already

sinking

in

bathwater . . .

I fished it out, and it

fell apart

in my hands.

I looked at Roger . . .

WEIR, YOU CAN STILL WEAR YOUR GREEN PAJAMAS.

"I can't just wear green," I complained. "I'll look like a **BIG cucumber!**"

Great, I get invited to Bella's party, and now I can't even go . . .

Then Sally stepped into the bathroom with an **"excellent idea."**

She pointed to the piles and piles of **toilet paper rolls** in the corner.

Sally is supposed to be the **clever** one, but this was the

worst idea ever!

"Sally, I'm **not** going as **toilet paper**!" I said.

Sally groaned. "No, we can wrap you with it, like a **mummy**!"

She picked up a roll and started **spinning** me around and around and around . . . and when I finally stopped whirling, I looked in the mirror and saw . . .

a really

COOL

mummy!

"Not bad," I said. "Thanks!"

So we're finally on our way to Bella's place, when we start running out of gas.

But instead of stopping at the first gas station we see, Dad wants to wait until we come across a **cheaper** one!

Sometimes Dad can be **just as thrifty** as Mom!

Can you guess what happened next?

We ran out of gas!

So Dad orders us all out, to help **push ››››** the car, while Granddad runs off to get us a can of gas.

First my **frog hat** gets destroyed, then our **car runs out of gas** on our way to the party . . .

What could be worse?

Granddad came back with gas, just as the rain stopped. But I no longer looked like a mummy . . .

I looked like a kid who'd been

FLUSHED down the toilet!

And my hands were covered in

FINKLES!

"What now?" I asked my genius sister.

I climbed back into the car. I looked in the trunk behind me and saw the mega bag of **chips** and the huge pack of **safety pins** that Roger had snuck into Mom's cart.

Roger's shopping had just given **me**

a BRILLIANT idea!

SNABBIT!

CHAPTER 7

I turned myself into a **vending machine**!

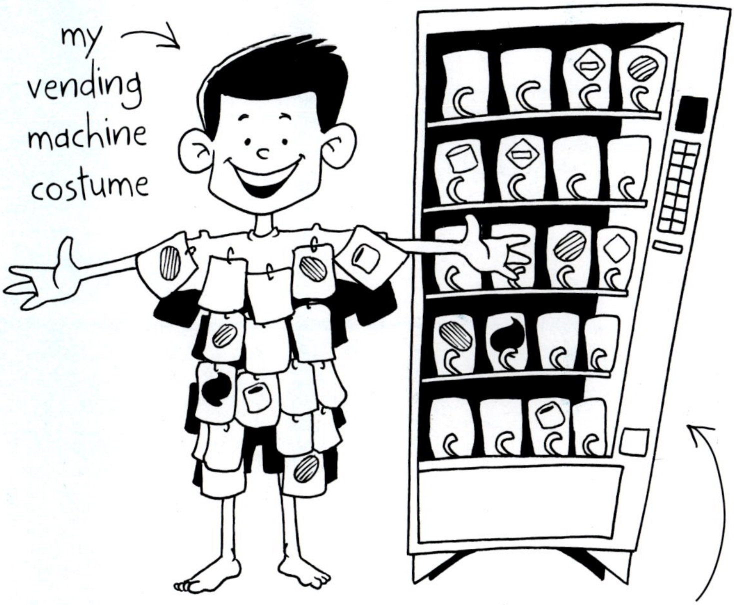

Everyone **loved it**, especially Bella's mom. She'd forgotten to pick up all the **party snacks**, so I'd arrived at just the right time . . .

MINE!
CHIPS!
OOH!
YUM!
MMM!
CHIPS!
YUM!
SALT AND VINEGAR!
MY FAVORITE!

THANKS!
THANKS!
THANKS, WEIR!
THANKS, WEIR!
THANKS!
THANKS!
YAY!

The only downside was that Toby Hogan tried to **pay for the chips** by putting a **coin** in my **ear**...

There was supposed to be a **magician** at the party, but he couldn't come because his **rabbit** had **eaten** his car keys.

But that didn't matter too much, because there was something at the party that turned out to be **much more fun** than a magician.

My crazy, weird family.

Granddad was up first to do some tricks. He pulled out his teeth . . .

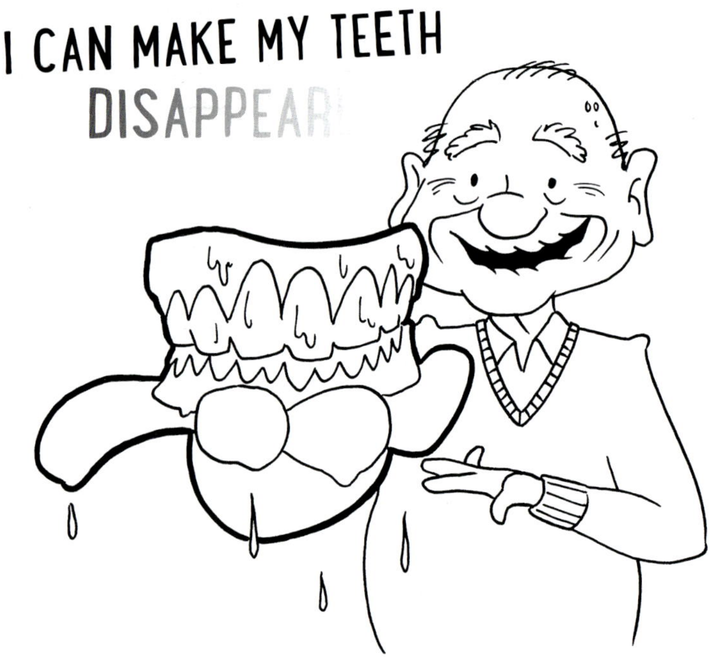

vanish

Then he made them ______!

WOW!

Next, he said,

WATCH MY MAGIC ELBOW.

TA-DA!

YAY!

Then **Dad** was up.

I started to **panic**. What was he going to do?

WHO WANTS TO
SEE ME
BURP
A SONG?

ME
ME
ME
ME
ME
ME

Dad burped his way through

Y TO YOU . . .'

Then some **music** came on the radio and **Dad started doing his**

horsey dance.

Soon **EVERYONE** was joining in.

Next, **Sally** started making some **cool balloon animals** for everyone.

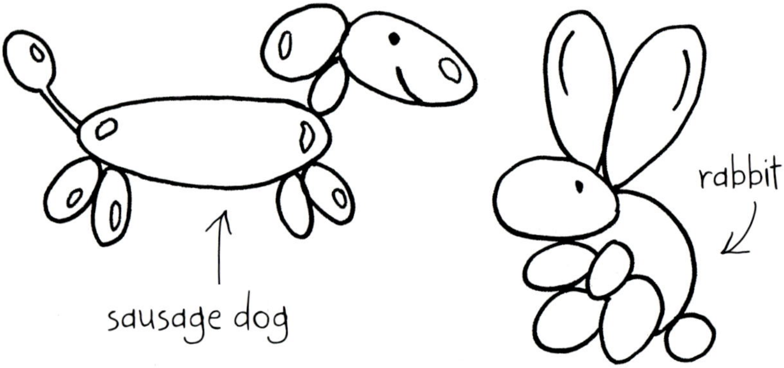

Then I made the only **balloon animal** that I knew how to.

Then I came up with

another GREAT idea!

I tied **my snake** to **Sally's rabbit** and made a **super-cool** animal.

THE BEST

CHAPTER 8

It was turning out to be a **great party**! I did a **BIG** drawing and we had a game of

pin the tail on the

donkey-potamus.

Roger helped Bella blow out her birthday candles, and Granddad **laughed** so loudly that his teeth

flew out

and landed in . . .

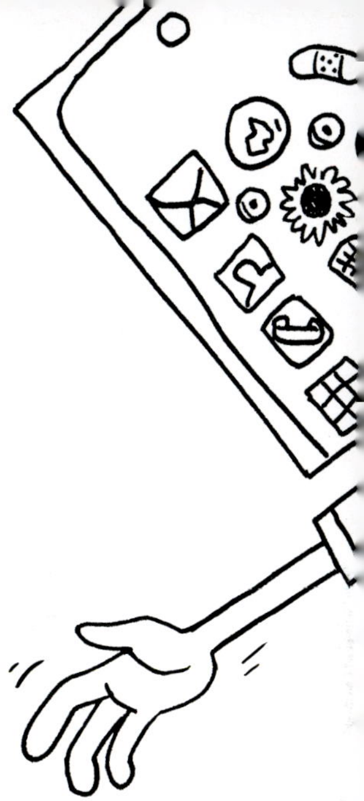

the candy bowl.

Henry thought they were **candy teeth** and was just about to **grab** them, when I **scooped** them up. "HENRY!

HENRY!!

HENRY!!!" I said.

"Huh?"

"Believe me, they're **NOT** as tasty as they look!"

Boy, that was close!

But before long, everyone was taking their **balloon animals** and saying goodbye.

Then I spotted Roger **dropping leftover cake into the fruit juice.**

I was trying to **scoop** the cake out, when Bella came up to us.

"He is **sooooo** cute," said Bella.

Cute? Roger?

I handed him to Mom.

"I'm really glad you came to my party, Weir," Bella added. "You know, your drawing of Clare yesterday was **really nice**."

"Thanks," I said.

"You drew me, on the bus, but I guess I'm not as nice-looking as her . . ."

HUH?

OH NO, YOU ARE!

I JUST . . .

IT WAS . . .

THE PROBLEM WAS YOUR GLASSES . . .

OH, YOU DON'T LIKE MY GLASSES?
NO, NO, I WAS WEARING YOUR GLASSES
. . . THAT'S WHY I DREW YOU FUNNY. I COULDN'T SEE PROPERLY!

"Oh!" said Bella.

"Hey, I almost forgot to give you this," I said, remembering the present in my pocket that I'd found for her at the zoo.

First, Bella opened the **card** I'd made her.

Bella blushed and gave me a **great big smile**.

I'm a bit short and I can't run very fast, but I'm **lucky** I can draw.

She opened the present next.

"Thanks, Weir," she said. "**You're the best**. And thanks for **saving** my party. It looked like it was going to be a disaster . . .

. . . UNTIL YOU AND YOUR FAMILY SHOWED UP.

UMM . . .
THANKS, BELLA.
MY FAMILY'S WAITING SO
I HAD BETTER GO . . .
SEE YOU AT
SCHOOL!

BYE, WEIR!

Phew. I'd made it through my **first birthday party** with my **new friends**.

And the **seventh-best-looking girl** in school just called me

THE BEST.

Me! Weir Do!

MORE TO COME!

For my three **boys** who helped me with this book . . .

FROM ANH

★ Henry's **funny-looking** mum and dad, based on drawings by **Xavier Do**

★ Henry's **strange** twin brothers, based on drawings by **Luc Do**

★ **Blockhead** the parrot's crazy habits, suggested by **Leon Do**

DEDICATIONS

FROM JULES

For Connor Maclean,
the **strongest**
kid I've ever known

bird

Weir Do's the new kid in school.
With an **unforgettable** name,
a **crazy** family, and some
seriously weird habits,
fitting in won't be easy . . .
but it will be **FUNNY!**

Book 1

GOT IT!

COLLECT THEM ALL!
YOU CAN NEVER HAVE TOO MANY WEIRDOS
WEIRDO 2
EVEN WEIRDER!
ANH DO
SCHOLASTIC
Book 2
GOT IT!
monkey
flying banana

SEE YA
SOON!